QUILTING
Travel Totes & Bags™

Designs by Jerry Shaw

HOUSE of
WHITE
BIRCHES
PUBLISHERS
SINCE 1947

Quilt Note

With more and more women traveling for work and for pleasure, the need for reliable luggage that is easily identifiable is more important than ever. This set of five bags will see you through a short weekend visit or a week's vacation at your favorite place to relax and enjoy life. The cosmetic bag with its nylon pockets, necessity bag with its clear plastic liner and jewelry bag with its drawstring pockets will help you find things easily as you travel. The large and small duffel bags are easy to pack and easy to handle as you travel by car or by air. Even better than that, when you travel by air you can spot your luggage easily on the carousels at airports.

Once you make a set for yourself and discover how much you enjoy using them, you'll want to make several sets to give as gifts at Christmastime. They also make perfect gifts for graduates or college students.

Table of Contents

General Instructions

The following list of instructions applies for use in making each of the five bags in the set.

- All seams are ⅜" unless otherwise instructed.
- Use an average stitch length for all sewing.
- To form zipper pulls, cut 6" strips of ⅜"-wide grosgrain ribbon, cutting the ends on a diagonal.
- Cut all bag pieces from single thickness of quilted fabric.
- Square one end of fabric and cut off selvage before beginning to cut out.
- Label pieces as you cut them out.
- Closed-bottom zippers work best, but separating zippers can be adapted.

Project Specifications
Large Bag: 17¼" x 7½" at bottom x 13½" high
Small Bag: 11¾" x 5" at bottom x 10¾" high
Cosmetic Bag: 9¼" x 8¼" x 6¾"
Necessity Bag: 12¼" x 9½" x 1½"
Jewelry Bag: 4" wide x 5" high

Fabric Requirements for Entire Set
Note: The sample projects used a quilted fabric with a stripe on one side and a print on the other.
- 3½ yards 42"-wide, double-sided quilted fabric
- 1½ yards 42"-wide, matching non-quilted fabric
- ¾ yard 58"-wide coordinating or white nylon fabric

Tools & Supplies for Entire Set
- All-purpose thread to match fabric
- Closed-bottom sport zippers: one 24", three 16", and two 14"
- 29" (⅝"-wide) hook-and-loop tape
- 25" (1½"-wide) coordinating grosgrain ribbon
- 96" (⅜"-wide) coordinating grosgrain ribbon for zipper pulls and jewelry bag drawstrings

- 12½" x 17½" rectangle medium-gauge, clear plastic for V in Necessity Bag
- Paper for patterns
- 6 (½") decorative flat buttons
- 1 (¼"-thick) plywood or plastic 7" x 15⅞" rectangle with rounded corners
- 1 (¼"-thick) plywood or plastic 4½ " x 11" rectangle with rounded-off corners
- Jar lid
- Zipper foot
- Basic sewing tools and supplies

Pattern Layout for Entire Set

Quilted Fabric
The layout shown in Figure 1 for the entire set worked well for the design on the fabric shown in the illustrations. Where matching was not feasible, the print on the backside of the quilted fabric was used as the right side. (The straps and the cosmetic bag back zipper strip.) Cut pieces as follows:

A—Large Bag: Cut two 25½" x 18" rectangles. Cut a 3¾" x 3¾" square out of two bottom corners referring to Figure 1 for cutout positioning.

B—Large Bag Inside Pockets: Cut two 25½" x 13¼" rectangles. Cut a 3¾" x 3¾" square out of two bottom corners referring to Figure 1 for cut-out positioning.

C—Large Bag Outside Pockets: Cut two 9¾" x 13¼" rectangles.

D—Large Bag Straps: Cut two 3" x 65" strips.

E—Small Bag: Cut two 17½" x 14" rectangles. Cut a 2⅝" x 2⅝" square out of two bottom corners referring to Figure 1 for cutout positioning.

F—Small Bag Inside Pockets: Cut two 17½" x 9¾" rectangles. Cut a 2⅝" x 2⅝" square out of two bottom corners referring to Figure 1 for cutout positioning.

G—Small Bag Outside Pockets: Cut two 7½" x 9¾" rectangles.

H—Small Bag Straps: Cut two 3" x 51" strips.

I—Cosmetic Bag Side Strip: Cut one 5" x 33" strip.

J—Cosmetic Bag Zipper Strips: Cut two 1½" x 27¾" strips.

K—Cosmetic Bag Back Zipper Strip: Cut one 2¾" x 6" strip.

L—Cosmetic Bag Top/Bottom: Cut two 9¾" x 8¾" rectangles.

M—Cosmetic Bag Strap: Cut one 3" x 7" strip.

N—Necessity Bag: Cut two 16" x 11" rectangles. (Use pattern to cut pieces; see project instructions.)

O—Necessity Bag Straps: Cut two 3" x 11¾" strips.

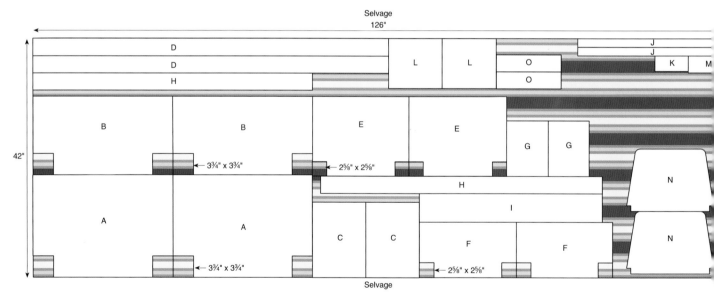

Figure 1
Cut quilted fabric for entire set as shown.

Non-quilted Fabric

See Figure 2 for layout of entire set on non-quilted fabric. Cut as follows:

A—Jewelry Bag Outside Half Circle: Cut two 14¾" half circles, adding ½" at straight edge. (Use pattern to cut pieces; see project instructions.)

B—Jewelry Bag Inside Circle: Cut two 10¾"-diameter circles.

C—Jewelry Bag Outside Circle: Cut one 14¾"-diameter circle.

S—Large Bag Bottom Board Pocket: Cut one 16½" x 18½" rectangle.

T—Small Bag Bottom Board Pocket: Cut one 11½" x 13½" rectangle.

Nylon Fabric

See Figure 3 for layout of entire set on nylon fabric. Cut as follows:

IN—Cosmetic Bag Sides: Cut one 5" x 33" strip (16¾" when placed on the fabric fold).

LN—Cosmetic Bag Top/Bottom: Cut two 9¾" x 8¾" rectangles.

NN—Necessity Bag: Cut two 16" x 11" rectangles. (Use pattern to cut pieces; see project instructions.)

UN—Cosmetic Bag Inside Pockets Strip: Cut one 5¾" x 50" strip (25" when placed on the fabric fold).

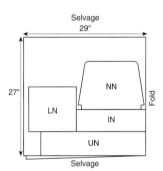

Figure 3
Cut nylon fabric for entire set as shown.

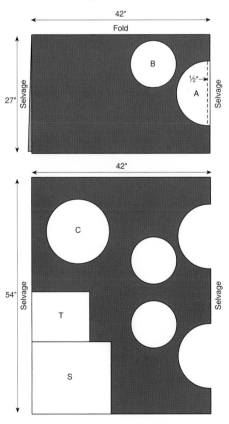

Figure 2
Cut non-quilted fabric for entire set as shown.

Large & Small Travel Bags

Travel in style with matching large and small travel bags.

Project Specifications
Large Bag: 17¼" x 7½" at bottom x 13½" high
Small Bag: 11¾" x 5" at bottom x 10¾" high

Fabric—Large and Small Travel Bags
- 3⅛ yards two-sided 42"-wide quilted fabric
- ½ yard 42"-wide non-quilted fabric

Large Travel Bag Alone
- 2⅛ yards two-sided 42"-wide quilted fabric
- ½ yard 42"-wide non-quilted fabric

Small Travel Bag Alone
- 1½ yards two-sided 42"-wide quilted fabric
- ⅜ yard 42"-wide non-quilted fabric

Tools & Supplies—Large Travel Bag
- 24" closed-bottom sport zipper
- 4" length ⅝"-wide hook-and-loop tape
- 6" length ⅜"-wide coordinating grosgrain ribbon for zipper pull
- 1 (¼"-thick) plywood or plastic 7" x 15⅞" rectangle with rounded corners
- Basic sewing tools and supplies

Tools & Supplies—Small Travel Bag
- 16" closed-bottom sport zipper
- 4" length ⅝"-wide hook-and-loop tape
- 6" length ⅜"-wide coordinating grosgrain ribbon for zipper pull
- 1 (¼"-thick) plywood or plastic 4½" x 11" rectangle with rounded corners

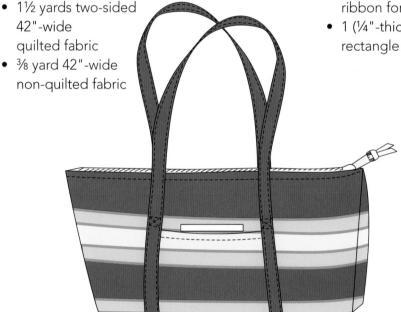

Large Travel Bag
Placement Diagram
17¼" x 7½" at bottom x 13½" high

Small Travel Bag
Placement Diagram
11¾" x 5" at bottom x 10¾" high

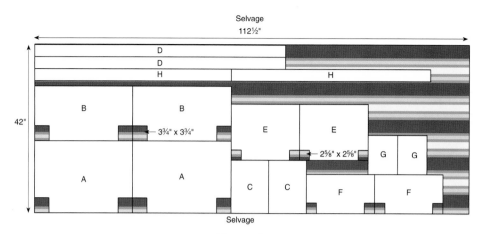

Figure 1
Cut pieces from quilted fabric as shown for large and small bags.

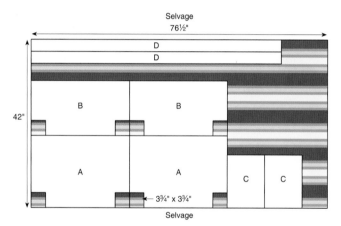

Figure 2
Cut pieces from quilted fabric as shown for large bag.

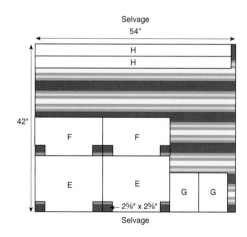

Figure 3
Cut pieces from quilted fabric
as shown for small bag.

Cutting Instructions for Quilted Fabrics

If making both the large and small bags, cut the following from the quilted fabric referring to Figure 1 for layout. If making only the large bag, cut referring to Figure 2 or only the small bag, cut referring to Figure 3.

A—Large Bag: Cut two 25½" x 18" rectangles. Cut a 3¾" x 3¾" square out of two bottom corners referring to Figure 1 or 2 for cutout positioning.

B—Large Bag Inside Pockets: Cut two 25½" x 13¼" rectangles. Cut a 3¾" x 3¾" square out of two bottom corners referring to Figure 1 or 2 for cutout positioning.

C—Large Bag Outside Pockets: Cut two 9¾" x 13¼" rectangles.

D—Large Bag Straps: Cut two 3" x 65" strips.

E—Small Bag: Cut two 17½" x 14" rectangles. Cut a 2⅝" x 2⅝" square out of two bottom corners referring to Figure 1 or 3 for cutout positioning.

F—Small Bag Inside Pockets: Cut two 17½" x 9¾" rectangles. Cut a 2⅝" x 2⅝" square out of two bottom corners referring to Figure 1 or 3 for cutout positioning.

G—Small Bag Outside Pockets: Cut two 7½" x 9¾" rectangles.

H—Small Bag Straps: Cut two 3" x 51" strips.

Non-Quilted Fabric

If making both the large and small bags, cut the following from the non-quilted fabric referring to Figure 4 for layout. If making only the large bag, cut referring to Figure 5 or only the small bag, cut referring to Figure 6.

Figure 6
Cut pieces from non-quilted fabric as shown for small bag.

S—Large Bag Bottom Board Pocket: Cut one 16½" x 18½" rectangle.

T—Small Bag Bottom Board Pocket: Cut one 11½" x 13½" rectangle.

Assembly Instructions

Note: *Instructions are given for the large bag. To complete the small bag, use piece E instead of A, F instead of B, G instead of C, H instead of D and T instead of S.*

1. Join ends of D strips to make a tube; press seams open.

2. Fold and press ⅜" to the front side on one long side and ½" on the other long side. Fold with fabric front sides together, matching pressed edges. Stitch ⅛" from open edge and ⅛" from folded edge as shown in Figure 7 to complete the strap; set aside.

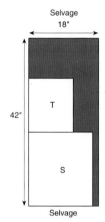

Figure 4
Cut pieces from non-quilted fabric as shown for large and small bags.

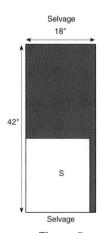

Figure 5
Cut pieces from non-quilted fabric as shown for large bag.

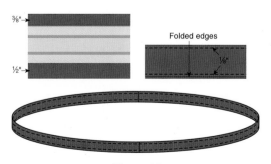

Figure 7
Fold and stitch ⅛" from each edge.

3. Using a serger or zigzag stitch, sew along the top edge of each B inside pocket and C outside pocket piece.

4. Using a zigzag stitch, center and stitch one strip of the hook tape to the right side of top edge of one C pocket hem.

5. Fold under a ¾" hem on the top edge of each B and C pocket piece; press. Stitch in place ⅝" from the folded edge as shown in Figure 8. ***Note:*** *Only one C outside pocket piece has hook tape.*

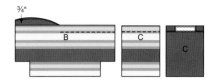

Figure 8
Hem B and C pockets as shown.

6. Center a C outside pocket on the outside of each A piece, matching bottom edges. Fold back the top edge of the C pocket with the hook tape. Align the loop tape on A with the hook tape on C; zigzag loop tape in place referring to Figure 9.

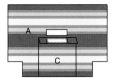

Figure 9
Align the loop tape with the hook tape; zigzag in place.

7. Pin B inside pockets in place on inside of A pieces, matching bottom raw edges and cutout corners. Machine-stitch across bottom of each panel ⅜" above the cutout corners as shown in Figure 10.

Figure 10
Machine-stitch across bottom of each panel ⅜" above the cutout corners.

8. Serge or zigzag all edges of each A/B panel, leaving cutout sections until last as shown in Figure 11.

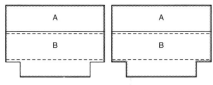

Figure 11
Stitch all edges of A/B panels, leaving cutout sections until last.

9. With right sides together, join the two A/B panels at the bottom edge as shown in Figure 12. Press seam open; stitch seam allowance down ¼" from seam line, again referring to Figure 12.

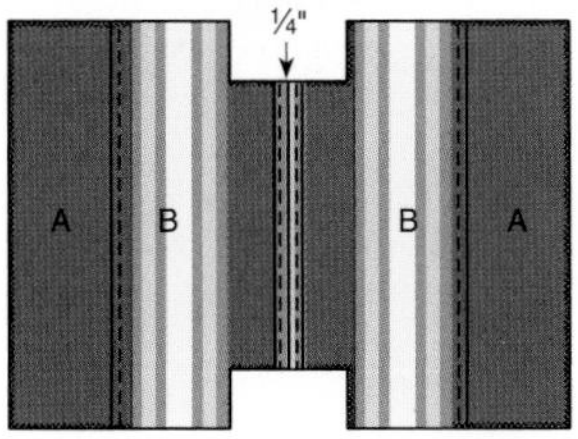

Figure 12
Join the 2 A/B panels at the bottom edge, press seam open and stitch seam allowance down ¼" from seam line.

10. Lay the stitched panel out flat right side up. Pin the strap in place, matching seams on strap with the bottom seam of the bag and overlapping the outside edges of pockets ⅜" as shown in Figure 13.

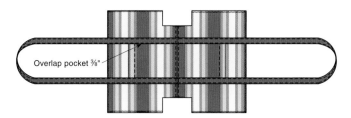

Figure 13
Place the strap, matching seams at bottom of the bag and overlapping the outside edges of pockets ⅜".

11. Stitch the strap in place, starting 1" above the top of the pocket. Sew a box with an X just above the pockets as shown in Figure 14. Do not stitch straps to bag above the X stitching. Reinforce pockets by using a zigzag stitch to make a ⅝"-long bar tack at the top of each pocket.

Figure 14
Stitch the strap in place, starting 1" above the pocket top edge. Sew a box with an X above the pockets.

12. Mark in ¾" from side edges at the end of each panel; open zipper and lay face down on one panel end even with top edge on the right side of the fabric, starting with the open end of zipper at the ¾" mark. Using a zipper foot, stitch a ⅜" seam between the ¾" marks to attach zipper tape.

13. Fold zipper tape to the inside and topstitch ¼" from top edge of panel; repeat on the other side of the zipper on the other end of panel. ***Note:*** *If using a separating zipper, sew a bar tack at the end to keep it from separating.*

14. With right sides together, pin side edges together and stitch as shown in Figure 15; press seams open. Fold zipper tape back on an angle at the zipper open end and stitch in place on topstitching line as shown in Figure 16.

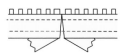

Figure 16
Fold zipper tape back on an angle at the zipper open end and stitch in place on topstitching line.

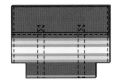

Figure 15
With right sides together, pin side seams together and stitch.

15. With right sides together, line up side seam with bottom seam on one end and stitch 3¾" (2½" for small bag) on both sides of the bottom/side seam as shown in Figure 17 to make square

bottom corners. Repeat on other end of bag. Turn the bag right side out.

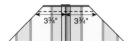

Figure 17
Stitch across the bottom on
both sides of seam to make
square bottom corners.

16. Fold the 6" strip of ⅜"-wide grosgrain ribbon in half, push folded edge through the zipper tab, forming a loop. Pull ends of ribbon through loop as shown in Figure 18. Cut ends diagonally.

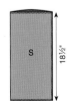

Figure 18
Create zipper loop
as shown.

17. Serge or zigzag one short edge of S; fold in half along length with right sides together. Serge side and bottom edges as shown in Figure 19. **Note:** *If using a zigzag stitch, sew a ¼" seam and then zigzag edges.*

Figure 19
Serge side and
bottom edges of S.

18. Turn S right side out; slip the plywood or plastic rectangle inside S. Turn extra material inside to cover the board for inside bag bottom. Insert in bag bottom to finish. ■

Necessity Bag

A clear plastic liner protects from accidental spills and allows you to locate your necessities with just a quick glance.

Project Specifications:
Bag size: 12¼" x 9½" x 1½"

Fabric:
- ½ yard 42"-wide, double-sided quilted fabric
- ⅜ yard 58"-wide coordinating or white nylon fabric

Tools & Supplies
- 12½" x 17½" rectangle medium-gauge, clear plastic for V
- 25" strip 1½"-wide coordinating grosgrain ribbon
- 2 (6") lengths ⅜"-wide coordinating grosgrain ribbon for zipper pulls
- 2 (16") closed-bottom sport zippers
- 21" length ⅝"-wide hook-and-loop tape
- 6 (½") decorative flat buttons
- 16" x 11" sheet of paper
- Basic sewing tools and supplies

Necessity Bag
Placement Diagram
12¼" x 9½" x 1½"

Pattern Layout & Cutting Instructions

1. Referring to Figure 1 to make a pattern for the N body of the bag, draw a line at the center from the top to the bottom on the 16" x 11" sheet of paper. Measure out 6¼" on both sides of the centerline on one 16" edge to make pattern top. Draw a straight line from these marks to the bottom corners; cut on these lines. The pattern should measure 12½" at the top and 16" at the bottom.

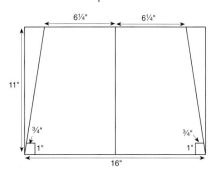

Figure 1
Make pattern for N as shown.

2. Again referring to Figure 1, measure up 1" from the bottom corner; draw a line ¾" across and 1" down. Cut out bottom corners; round top corners to complete paper pattern for N.

3. Referring to Figure 2, cut two N pieces from the quilted fabric. Using the N pattern, cut two NN pieces from the nylon fabric.

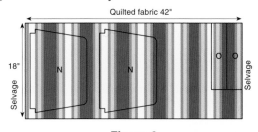

Figure 2
Cut pieces as shown.

4. Cut two 3" x 11¾" O strips from quilted fabric for the straps, again referring to Figure 2.

5. Cut the 25" strip of 1½"-wide coordinating grosgrain ribbon in half to make two 12½" lengths. Fold each piece in half along length to make a double-layered strip as shown in Figure 3.

Figure 3
Fold each piece in half
along length to make a
double-layered strip.

6. Cut two 10½" lengths of hook-and-loop tape.

Assembly Instructions

1. Serge or zigzag ends of each O strap.

2. Fold and press ⅜" to the front side on one long edge of each O strap; fold ½" on the other long edge.

3. Fold each O strap in half along length with front sides together, matching folded edges; stitch ⅛" from open edges of each strap. Stitch ⅛" from the folded edge.

4. Enclose both 12½" ends of the V plastic piece with a length of folded grosgrain ribbon as shown in Figure 4; stitch in place close to edge of ribbon. *Hint: When working with the plastic, lay paper under the plastic next to the presser foot to help the plastic glide through.*

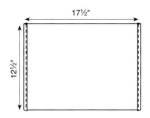

Figure 4
Enclose both 12½" ends of the V
plastic piece with a matching length
of folded grosgrain ribbon.

5. Center one hook strip of the hook-and-loop tape on the underside of each grosgrain end of V referring to Figure 5; stitch in place, sewing over the ribbon stitching. Zigzag-stitch the ends and along the ribbon fold, again referring to Figure 5.

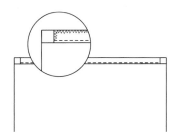

Figure 5
Center 1 hook strip of
the hook-and-loop tape
on the underside of
each grosgrain ribbon.

6. Center one loop strip 1⅞" down from the top, on the right side of NN; stitch in place using a zigzag stitch referring to Figure 6.

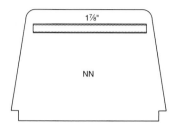

Figure 6
Center and zigzag-stitch 1 loop strip 1⅞" down from the top, on the right side of NN.

7. Referring to Figure 7, center O straps on the right side of each N piece along the top edges, leaving 3½" between ends; stitch in place using a ¼" seam allowance.

Figure 7
Center O strap on the right side of N piece along the top edges, leaving 3½" between ends; stitch in place using a ¼" seam allowance.

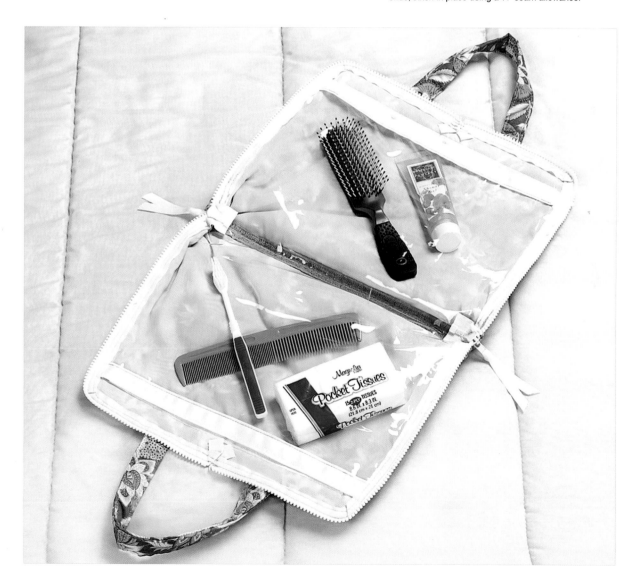

8. Pin right sides of NN lining to right sides of each N piece; stitch around each layered panel, leaving the bottom edges open as shown in Figure 8.

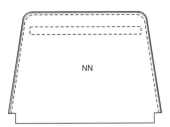

Figure 8
Stitch around each
layered panel, leaving
the bottom edges open.

9. Clip curved corners at the top edges and turn layered panels right side out; press seams flat.

10. Serge or zigzag bottom edges of N and NN together; repeat on cutout corners.

11. Referring to Figure 9, sew the ½" decorative flat buttons through all layers on the outside of the N/NN panels directly over the loop strip on the inside, with one button in the center of the loop strip and the others 2½" away on each side. ***Note:*** *The buttons will anchor the lining to the outside of the bag.*

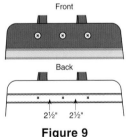

Front

Back

2½" 2½"

Figure 9
Position and sew buttons
in place as shown.

12. Pin layered panels together on the bottom and cutout edges with right sides together; stitch. Press seam open; topstitch each side of seam in place.

13. To form the bottom corner, pin the right sides together, placing the sides ¼" from the bottom seam as shown in Figure 10. ***Note:*** *This gives you a ½" opening for the zipper.* Stitch across ⅜" from edge, again referring to Figure 10.

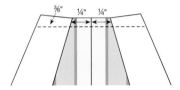

⅜"   ¼"   ¼"

Figure 10
Pin the right sides together, placing the
sides ¼" from the bottom seam to make
bottom corner; stitch ⅜" from edge.

14. Insert V plastic pockets piece, aligning the hook tape with the loop tape. Trim the grosgrain ribbon and plastic that may extend beyond the sides at the top.

15. Open both zippers and center them face down at the top edge on the inside of the layered panel, folding back the end of zipper tape as shown in Figure 11.

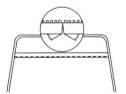

Figure 11
Center zippers face down
on the inside of panel;
fold back end of tape.

16. Lay zipper teeth along edges of layered panel, encasing edges of plastic with zipper tape. Place the closed ends of the zippers at the bag bottom and extend remaining zipper sides onto the other side of the bag. Using a zipper foot, sew the zippers in on one bag side only; sew a second row of stitching ³⁄₁₆" from the first row as shown in Figure 12. Repeat to insert the other side of the zippers on the other side of the bag, closing the zippers at the bottom before starting.

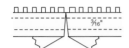

Figure 12
Sew the zippers in; sew ³⁄₁₆"
from first line of stitching.

17. Using a sheet of paper again to help the plastic slide through the machine, sew across the plastic pockets piece along the bottom seam of bag with the fabric side up, sewing to the outside

edges as close as possible. ***Note:*** *If you used a separating zipper, sew a bar tack at the end to keep it together.*

Figure 13
Create zipper loop
as shown.

18. Fold the 6" strip of ³⁄₈"-wide coordinating grosgrain ribbon in half across width and push folded edge through the zipper tab, forming a loop; pull the ends of the ribbon through the loop referring to Figure 13. Trim ends diagonally to finish. ■

Jewelry Bag

A pocketed drawstring bag is the perfect travel container for your special jewelry.

Project Specifications
Bag Size: 4" wide x 5" high

Fabric
- ¾ yard 42"-wide non-quilted fabric

Tools & Supplies
- 3 paper circle patterns—one each 14¾" diameter for A and C, 10¾" diameter for B and 4" diameter for D
- 2 (30") lengths of ⅜"-wide coordinating grosgrain ribbon
- Basic sewing tools and supplies

Cutting
1. Fold fabric in half across the 27" length.

2. Fold the A/C paper pattern in half; cut two half pieces from fabric for A, adding ½" at the folded edge for seam as shown in Figure 1.

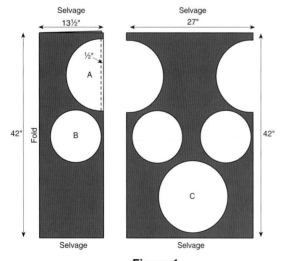

Figure 1
Cut A, B and C pieces as shown.

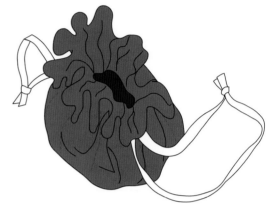

Jewelry Bag
Placement Diagram
4" wide x 5" high

3. Cut two B circles from folded fabric, again referring to Figure 1. Unfold fabric and the A/C paper pattern and cut one C circle, again referring to Figure 1.

Assembly Instructions
1. Serge or zigzag along the straight edges of each A piece.

2. Pin A pieces with right sides together; make a mark 1⅜" and ¾" on each end of the straight edge as shown in Figure 2.

Figure 2
Mark straight edge of layered A pieces as shown.

3. Referring to Figure 3, stitch to first marked line using a ½" seam allowance and securing stitching at the beginning and end. Leave the ¾" opening and begin stitching at the next marking, securing stitching at the beginning and end. Stitch to the next marked line, leave the ¾" opening and stitch to the end; press the seam open.

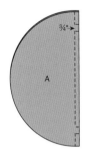

Figure 3
Stitch as shown,
leaving ¾" openings.

4. Pin the C circle right sides together with the stitched A circle; sew a ⅜" seam all around, leaving a 3" opening for turning. Clip curved edges; finger-press seam open. Turn right side out; hand-stitch opening closed; press flat.

5. Sew around outside 1" from the edge and then again at 1¾" as shown in Figure 4; set aside.

6. Pin B circles right sides together and stitch a ⅜" seam all around, leaving a 2" opening for turning; clip curved edges. Finger-press seam open; turn right side out. Hand-stitch opening closed; press flat.

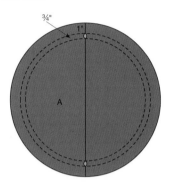

Figure 4
Sew around outside 1"
from the edge and then
again at 1¾".

7. Center the stitched B circles on top of the stitched A unit with seamed A side down. Pin through center of B on the seam line of the stitched A unit.

8. Referring to Figure 5, mark lines on circle to make eight equal sections. Center and mark a 4" D circle, again referring to Figure 5. Sew on the marked D circle line and on each marked line, securing stitching at the beginning and end to make eight pockets.

Figure 5
Mark lines on circle to make
8 equal openings. Center
and mark a D circle.

9. Thread the two 30" lengths of ⅜"-wide grosgrain ribbon through the openings in the seams of the A circle. Start them simultaneously, one on each side and pull each one all the way around to its beginning. Tie the two ends of one length together to secure; repeat with ends of second length. ■

Cosmetic Bag

Nylon pockets hold cosmetic items inside this quilted bag.

Project Specifications
Bag Size: Approximately 9¼" x 8¼" x 6¾"

Fabric
- ½ yard 42"-wide, double-sided quilted fabric
- ½ yard 58"-wide coordinating or white nylon fabric

Tools & Supplies
- 2 (6") strips ⅜"-wide coordinating grosgrain ribbon for zipper pulls
- 2 (14") closed-bottom sport zippers
- Jar lid
- Basic sewing tools and supplies

Pattern Layout and Cutting Instructions
Note: *Refer to Figure 1 for all cutting layouts.*

1. Cut two 9¾" x 8¾" rectangles each from the quilted (L) and nylon (LN) fabrics. Layer the L rectangles right sides together; place the LN rectangles between the L rectangles; pin layers to hold. Use a jar lid to round corners.

2. Cut one 5" x 33" side strip from the quilted (I) and nylon (IN) fabrics.

3. Cut two J zipper strips 1½" x 27¾", one K back zipper strip 2¾" x 6" and one M strap 3" x 7" from the quilted fabric.

4. Cut one UN inside pocket strip 5½" x 50" from the nylon fabric (5½" x 25" when cut on fold).

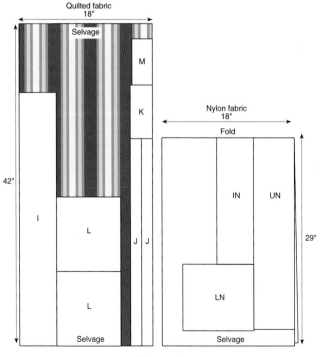

Figure 1
Cut pieces as shown.

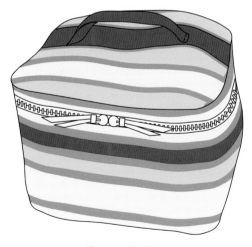

Cosmetic Bag
Placement Diagram
9¼" x 8¼" x 6¾"

Assembly Instructions

Note: *Use a ⅜" seam allowance throughout unless otherwise directed.*

1. Fold both long edges of the UN nylon pocket strip under ½"; press. Fold under another ½"; press. Stitch to hem; set aside.

2. Serge or zigzag the 3" ends of the M strap. Fold ⅜" to the front side on one 7" edge and ⅛" on the other 7" edge; press. Fold the strip in half along length with front sides together, matching pressed edges; stitch ⅛" from the edge on both 7" sides.

3. Referring to Figure 2, center the serged or stitched end of the M strap 2¼" from the edge on the right side of one 8¾" edge of one L piece. Stitch across end; fold M back over itself and stitch again to enclose the serged end as shown in Figure 3. Repeat with the other end of the M strap, measuring in from the other end of L.

Figure 2
Center 1 serged or stitched end of the
M strap 2¼" from the edge of the right
side of one 8¾" edge of 1 L piece.

Figure 3
Stitch across end; fold M back
over itself and stitch again to
enclose the serged end.

4. Pin LN to the wrong side of L; serge or zigzag together around all sides with LN on top as you stitch. Repeat with the second L and LN pieces and the I and IN side strips.

5. To mark pocket sections on the I/IN strip, fold the strip in half across the width; fold each half in half and each quarter in half to make eight equal-size sections; press the folds on the I/IN strip. Unfold strip; place a pin at the top and bottom edges at each pressed fold line. Repeat with the UN nylon pocket strip.

6. Place the UN pocket strip ½" in from one long edge on the nylon side of the I/IN strip. Align the pinned sections and stitch in place on the pressed fold lines to make pockets as shown in Figure 4, sewing from top to bottom of the I/IN strip and securing beginning and end of seam.

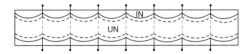

Figure 4
Align the pinned sections and stitch in place
on the pressed fold lines to make pockets.

7. Serge or zigzag the short ends of the side/pocket strip.

8. With right sides together, stitch the short ends of the side/pocket strip together to make a tube; press seam open and topstitch on each side of the seam.

9. Pin L/LN bottom piece to the stitched tube with right sides together, matching corners of L/LN to seam lines between pockets on side/pocket strip and centering the back seam of side/pocket strip on one long side of the L/LN piece referring to Figure 5. **Note:** *This places two pockets on each side of L/LN.* Stitch pieces together using a ¼" seam allowance; set aside.

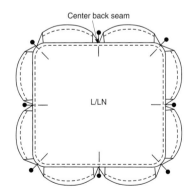

Figure 5
Center the back seam on the
long side of the L/LN piece.

10. Serge or zigzag all edges of the J zipper strips. Fold strips in half across width and press to mark the center. Fold zipper tape end back toward the right side of the zipper at an angle as shown in Figure 6.

Figure 6
Fold zipper tape end back
toward the right side of
the zipper at an angle.

11. Referring to Figure 7 and starting at the center, pin zipper face down to the right side of zipper strip. **Note:** *The zipper tape should be even with serged or zigzagged edge. Zipper will extend beyond end of strip.* Stitch in place ⅜" from serged edge, stitching to the end of the J zipper strip. Repeat with second zipper on the other end of the J zipper strip, starting the zipper at the center of the strip.

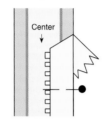

Figure 7
Pin zipper face down to
the right side of zipper
strip, starting at the center.

12. Fold zipper tape toward inside of strip and topstitch ¼" in from top fabric edge as shown in Figure 8.

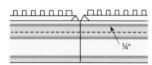

Figure 8
Fold zipper tape toward
strip and topstitch at ¼".

13. Serge or zigzag all edges of K. Place front side of J zipper strip on the backside of the K back zipper strip; stitch together to make a tube as shown in Figure 9. Press seams toward K; topstitch ¼" inside K to hold seams in place.

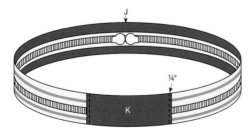

Figure 9
Stitch J and K together
to make a tube.

14. Fold J/K zipper strip in half with K piece centered in fold and in half again; mark folds with pins. Pin right side of L/LN to the right side of the J/K zipper strip, matching the pins on the J/K strip to the centers of the L/LN sides. Stitch with J/K zipper strip on top using a ¼" seam allowance.

15. Place pins at the corners and side centers of the bag top and bottom units. Turn the bag bottom unit wrong side out and bag top unit right side out. Open zippers and slip top unit into bottom unit with right sides together, matching pins; pin through all layers to hold. **Note:** *Be sure to align zipper opening with center front.* Stitch a ¼" seam; turn right side out. Press seam toward bottom unit; topstitch to hold.

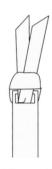

Figure 10
Create zipper
loop as shown.

16. Fold each ⅜"-wide strip of grosgrain ribbon in half across width. Push one piece through each zipper tab forming a loop; pull cut edges of grosgrain through the loop referring to Figure 10. Trim ends diagonally to finish. ■

Embroidery Stitch Guide

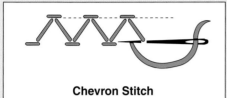

Chevron Stitch

Fly Stitch

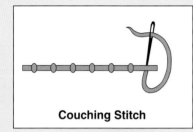

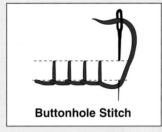

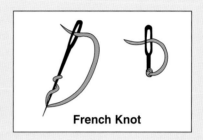

Couching Stitch

Buttonhole Stitch

French Knot

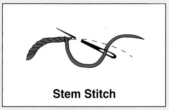

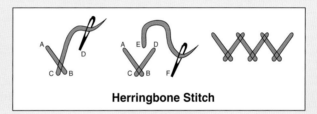

Stem Stitch

Herringbone Stitch

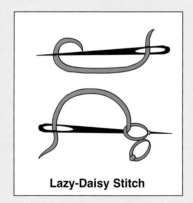

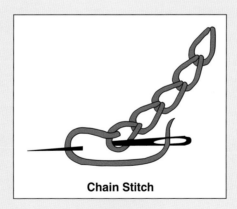

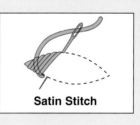

Satin Stitch

Lazy-Daisy Stitch

Chain Stitch

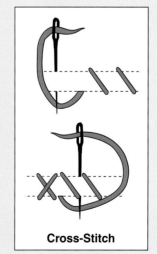

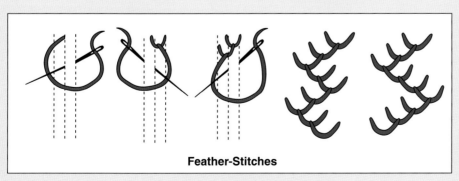

Feather-Stitches

Cross-Stitch

Metric Conversion Charts

Metric Conversions

U.S. Measurement		Multiplied by		Metric Measurement
yards	x	.9144	=	meters (m)
yards	x	91.44	=	centimeters (cm)
inches	x	2.54	=	centimeters (cm)
inches	x	25.40	=	millimeters (mm)
inches	x	.0254	=	meters (m)

Metric Measurement		Multiplied by		U.S. Measurement
centimeters	x	.3937	=	inches
meters	x	1.0936	=	yards

Standard Equivalents

U.S. Measurement		Metric Measurement		
1/8 inch	=	3.20 mm	=	0.32 cm
1/4 inch	=	6.35 mm	=	0.635 cm
3/8 inch	=	9.50 mm	=	0.95 cm
1/2 inch	=	12.70 mm	=	1.27 cm
5/8 inch	=	15.90 mm	=	1.59 cm
3/4 inch	=	19.10 mm	=	1.91 cm
7/8 inch	=	22.20 mm	=	2.22 cm
1 inch	=	25.40 mm	=	2.54 cm
1/8 yard	=	11.43 cm	=	0.11 m
1/4 yard	=	22.86 cm	=	0.23 m
3/8 yard	=	34.29 cm	=	0.34 m
1/2 yard	=	45.72 cm	=	0.46 m
5/8 yard	=	57.15 cm	=	0.57 m
3/4 yard	=	68.58 cm	=	0.69 m
7/8 yard	=	80.00 cm	=	0.80 m
1 yard	=	91.44 cm	=	0.91 m

U.S. Measurement		Metric Measurement		
1 1/8 yard	=	102.87 cm	=	1.03 m
1 1/4 yard	=	114.30 cm	=	1.14 m
1 3/8 yard	=	125.73 cm	=	1.26 m
1 1/2 yard	=	137.16 cm	=	1.37 m
1 5/8 yard	=	148.59 cm	=	1.49 m
1 3/4 yard	=	160.02 cm	=	1.60 m
1 7/8 yard	=	171.44 cm	=	1.71 m
2 yards	=	182.88 cm	=	1.83 m
2 1/8 yards	=	194.31 cm	=	1.94 m
2 1/4 yards	=	205.74 cm	=	2.06 m
2 3/8 yards	=	217.17 cm	=	2.17 m
2 1/2 yards	=	228.60 cm	=	2.29 m
2 5/8 yards	=	240.03 cm	=	2.40 m
2 3/4 yards	=	251.46 cm	=	2.51 m
2 7/8 yards	=	262.88 cm	=	2.63 m
3 yards	=	274.32 cm	=	2.74 m
3 1/8 yards	=	285.75 cm	=	2.86 m
3 1/4 yards	=	297.18 cm	=	2.97 m
3 3/8 yards	=	308.61 cm	=	3.09 m
3 1/2 yards	=	320.04 cm	=	3.20 m
3 5/8 yards	=	331.47 cm	=	3.31 m
3 3/4 yards	=	342.90 cm	=	3.43 m
3 7/8 yards	=	354.32 cm	=	3.54 m
4 yards	=	365.76 cm	=	3.66 m
4 1/8 yards	=	377.19 cm	=	3.77 m
4 1/4 yards	=	388.62 cm	=	3.89 m
4 3/8 yards	=	400.05 cm	=	4.00 m
4 1/2 yards	=	411.48 cm	=	4.11 m
4 5/8 yards	=	422.91 cm	=	4.23 m
4 3/4 yards	=	434.34 cm	=	4.34 m
4 7/8 yards	=	445.76 cm	=	4.46 m
5 yards	=	457.20 cm	=	4.57 m

Meet the Designer

Jerry Shaw

Jerry Shaw has rediscovered her passion for sewing after recently retiring from teaching family and consumer sciences. She has been sewing since the age of 10, when she made a complete wardrobe for her doll, sewing everything by hand.

Since retiring, she has created a business, Purses by Jerry, out of her home near Bluffton, Ind., and is enjoying every aspect of it.

Jerry has been married for 42 years, has four beautiful daughters, two wonderful sons-in-law and four adorable grandchildren. When Jerry isn't sewing or spending time with her family, she enjoys reading, crocheting, flower gardening and traveling.

Her interest in traveling began years ago when she accompanied her husband, Ray, to Germany while he was serving five years in the Army. Since that time, she has traveled to various places within the continental United States, Hawaii and Alaska, as well as to Russia and Lithuania. Her recent travels included a two-day bus trip to Dover, Ohio, where she visited an Amish community and the Warther wood carving factory and museum.

E-mail: Customer_Service@whitebirches.com

HOUSE of WHITE BIRCHES
PUBLISHERS SINCE 1947

Travel Totes & Bags is published by House of White Birches, 306 East Parr Road, Berne, IN 46711, telephone (260) 589-4000. Printed in USA. Copyright © 2004 House of White Birches.

RETAILERS: If you would like to carry this pattern book or any other House of White Birches publications, call the Wholesale Department at Annie's Attic to set up a direct account: (903) 636-4303. Also, request a complete listing of publications available from House of White Birches.

Every effort has been made to ensure that the instructions in this pattern book are complete and accurate. We cannot, however, take responsibility for human error, typographical mistakes or variations in individual work.

ISBN: 1-59217-031-5
3 4 5 6 7 8 9

STAFF

Editors: Jeanne Stauffer, Sandra L. Hatch
Associate Editor: Dianne Schmidt
Technical Artist: Connie Rand
Copy Editors: Michelle Beck, Nicki Lehman, Conor Allen, Sue Harvey
Art Director: Brad Snow
Assistant Art Director: Karen Allen
Graphic Arts Supervisor: Ronda Bechinski
Graphic Artist: Glenda Chamberlain
Photography: Tammy Christian, Christena Green, Matt Owen, Carl Clark
Photo Stylist: Tammy Nussbaum